For my big sister, the REAL Jana Banana - ma

Dedicated to Camille, Vincent and K.K.--McKay's whole world - mf

Text copyright © 2025 by Mike Atwood

Illustrations copyright © 2025 by McKay Fife

All rights reserved. No part of this book may be reproduced or utilized in any form or by any means, electronic or mechanical, including photocopying, recording, or by any information storage and retrieval system, without permission in writing from the author.

Illustrations for the book were rendered digitally.

Summary: A young girl with a wild imagination discovers that she can make her thoughts become reality.

Written by
Mike Atwood

Illustrated by
McKay Fife

Jana Banana

Jana Banana was one of a kind –
a fun-loving girl with a mischievous mind.
And that mind of hers thought the most wonderful thoughts
until **ONE** little thought put her in a tough spot!

Have you ever wondered how cool it would be,
to fly like a bird, or be a fish in the sea?
Well, Jana Banana had thoughts like these too;
but when **SHE** thought them up, then they really came true!

The first time it happened was when she was five.
She was in the back seat, but she wanted to drive –
and the next thing she knew she was at the wheel steering,
while her mom, in surprise, began clapping and cheering.

Most moms wouldn't do that, but this mom was rare,
and while Jana was driving, her mom did her hair –
and said, "Jana, this car is too little for us –
I wish it was BIG, like a van or a bus."

Well, it didn't take long for that thought to arrive
in Jana's own mind - now she wanted to drive
in a big family van with a few rows of seats,
and a bed in the back, with some real comfy sheets,
so that when they took road trips - as families will do,
they could drive all day long, and then nap in there too.

And no sooner had this thought formed in her head,
than Jana Banana was asleep in that bed –
her Mom driving home, with her hair in the breeze,
to go surprise Dad with a new set of keys.

Now this was the first JANA THOUGHT that came true,
but she had many more, and I'll share them with you.
The next came in third grade, while in Social Studies,
day-dreaming of what it was like to have buddies,
like Sacagawea or Lewis and Clarke,
when suddenly everything got really dark...

Then, Jana was sitting near campfire light,
As Sacagawea sang songs in the night
about mountains and rivers, and great grizzly bears,
in a language not Jana's – but she was aware
that she understood while the young mother sang
of that great Western trail… 'til the school bell rang.

Then Jana was 'POOF' sitting back in her class,
singing perfect Shoshone with plenty of sass.
So her teacher and classmates thought it would be best
that she see the school nurse and go get a brain test.

But Jana was wise and from then on, she knew,
that to know someone well, you must walk in their shoes.
So when studying Algebra, English, or Science,
she'd go visit Shakespeare, then form an alliance
with Newton or Einstein, to whom she declared
that her time-jumping mind was indeed m c squared.

While Jana enjoyed playing mind games alone,
she also had fun with her siblings at home.
She'd act like a lioness, plagued with the toots,
that was chasing her kittens, whose laughter and hoots
would make her believe in the game, and like that -

She became the most silly (and stinky) big cat!

When this thought came true, her mind started to soar,
and her thoughts became BIGGER than ever before!
"Hmmm... What if I ruled my own kingdom?" she pondered,
and quickly her thoughts multiplied and then wandered.

Soon you will see Jana's mind ran amuck, and this time her thoughts got her terribly stuck

She had sat all day long as a Queen on her throne, surrounded by people, but feeling alone.
She thought, "Do these folks in my kingdom pretend that I'm a good Queen, and they want to be friends?"

And then a thought came, and it wasn't so nice.
In fact, it was bad, made her heart cold as ice.
She thought, "If my subjects don't like me, I guess,
I'm a terrible ruler, and maybe it's best –

That I give up my throne and stop being their Queen -
let someone else do it, I'm leaving this scene!"

So she went on the run, far away from the land,
(since her day as the Queen hadn't turned out as planned).
She tried to escape her bad thoughts and not face them,
and started to think some **NEW** thoughts to erase 'em.

She thought of a unicorn,
but then got quite bored
of just prancing around,
so she thought of a sword.

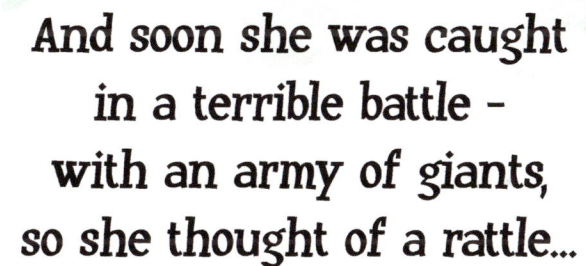

And soon she was caught
in a terrible battle -
with an army of giants,
so she thought of a rattle...

...since babies seemed safer -
but, for Heaven's sake,
she found herself wrapped in
the coils of a snake!

And then 'POOF' she was nothing – or at least very small.

As small as a speck or a dot or a gnat . . .
Now the world looked much bigger from where she was at.

The grass was a jungle, the bugs giant beasts
who seemed to think Jana would make a good feast.

But what even was she? Or who, when, or where?
Did anyone know she was gone? Did they care?

And how did she get in this terrible mess?
What started it all? Well, I think YOU can guess.

When Jana Banana decided to run
from her not-so-nice thought, then the bad thought had won.
So there was just one thing that Jana could do:
It was talking her thoughts out of **ALL** coming true.

Then 'POOF' she was back in her castle as Queen,
and remembered how worried her thoughts had once been.
So she said, "Listen brain, I'm the Queen of you too!
Stop making me feel like the gum on my shoe!
My subjects might love me, or maybe they won't -
But I can love me, even if others don't."

Then just at that moment, she looked in the eyes,
of her subjects – and now she could see with surprise
that they really did love her, their kind, gracious leader,
and they wanted to dance with her, hug her, and feed her.

When the sun finally set on that very strange day, Jana saw how her thoughts could get carried away to good or bad places, but she was in charge of feeding those thoughts, or of letting them starve.

She learned that her thoughts could create how she'd feel,
And when acting on feelings - those thoughts became real.
So she said to herself: "Listen, I'm good enough!"
I'm in charge of YOU, brain! You don't like it, then TOUGH!"

So now when she has a big thought she can choose,
to let the thought win, or to let the thought lose.

That never stops her from creating new schemes . . .

And it shouldn't stop you, so
Go dream some big dreams!

The End.

About the Author

Mike Atwood has been writing stories and sharing them with friends and family since kindergarten. *Jana Banana* is loosely based on some of the stories and adventures from growing up with his six siblings, including his big sister, the real Jana Banana.

Mike graduated from the University of Lethbridge with a BFA in New Media and worked as a graphic designer for a number of years before changing his artistic canvas to teeth (he's a dentist now). Mike lives in Southern Alberta, Canada with his wife and children.

You can scan the QR code to follow the author on Facebook.

About the Illustrator

McKay Fife is an illustrator & character designer from Boise, Idaho in the USA. When he isn't drawing, watching captivating films, playing his favorite video games or listening to niche indie rock, he's probably doing all of the above with his perfect wife, his new baby boy, and crazy dog who never gets bored.

McKay has a degree in Illustration with an Emphasis in Entertainment form Brigham Young University-Idaho, and teaches art there part time.

Check out more of McKay's art at metroidmckay_art.artstation.com

www.ingramcontent.com/pod-product-compliance
Lightning Source LLC
LaVergne TN
LVHW072357110526
838202LV00104B/2622